Life And Services Of David French Boyd

Andrew Augustus Gunby

In the interest of creating a more extensive selection of rare historical book reprints, we have chosen to reproduce this title even though it may possibly have occasional imperfections such as missing and blurred pages, missing text, poor pictures, markings, dark backgrounds and other reproduction issues beyond our control. Because this work is culturally important, we have made it available as a part of our commitment to protecting, preserving and promoting the world's literature. Thank you for your understanding.

UNIVERSITY BULLETIN.

| SERIES II. | JUNE, 1904. | No. 2. |

LOUISIANA STATE UNIVERSITY

BATON ROUGE, LA.

LIFE AND SERVICES
.. OF ..
DAVID FRENCH BOYD

PUBLISHED BY THE LOUISIANA STATE UNIVERSITY AT BATON ROUGE.
ISSUED IN MAY, JUNE, JULY AND AUGUST.

Entered July 1, 1903, at Baton Rouge, La., as second class matter,
under Act of Congress of July 16, 1894.

NEW ORLEANS:
T. H. THOMASON.
1904

COL. D. F. BOYD AND HIS LIFE-WORK.

AN ADDRESS DELIVERED BY A. A. GUNBY AT THE LAYING OF THE CORNER STONE OF THE ALUMNI MEMORIAL HALL, ERECTED IN HONOR OF DAVID FRENCH BOYD, ON THE GROUNDS OF THE LOUISIANA STATE UNIVERSITY AND AGRICULTURAL AND MECHANICAL COLLEGE, AT BATON ROUGE, LOUISIANA, MAY THE THIRTY-FIRST, NINETEEN HUNDRED AND FOUR.

Tacitus, the most philosophical and instructive historian of ancient times, in his introduction to the life of Agricola, justly remarks that biography is esteemed only when great and splendid virtue has been able to surmount those two pernicious vices, insensibility to merit, on the one hand, and envy, on the other.

If I did not feel that those two vices are absent from this community and this State, as far as they concern the illustrious man of whom I speak to-day, if I did not believe that envy's sharp and bitter tooth has long ago been turned away from him, and that everybody here present is already sensible of his great and splendid virtues, I would not have obeyed the mandate of the Alumni Association who commissioned me to speak for them and explain why they determined to erect this noble Memorial Hall in memory of Colonel David French Boyd, who never held any position of power, who commanded no great armies, who gained no great victories, who was never greeted by the shout of triumph, nor heard "The applause of listening senates." His only vocation was teaching. Louisiana has had many illustrious sons, presidents, senators, generals, diplomats, statesmen, artists and captains of industry. Yet none of them after death, has been honored with such a monument, as this within her borders. Why should D. F. Boyd be honored above all other Louisianians? I am here to tell you why. I will endeavor to draw a picture of his life, a plain and honest picture, foregoing all comment, indulging in no panegyric, letting the facts speak for themselves; facts which are more eloquent than any flights of rhetoric or figures of speech. I must restrain all words of partial praise and all feelings of personal friendship and admiration that might well up in my bosom in speaking of one to whom I owe so much. I must deprive myself of the pleasure of dwelling on the fine traits of his personality, his buoyant humor, his genial bonhommie, his universal comradeship that quickened the pulse of life around him. I must leave to others the task of preserving a record of his vast scholarship, his habits of industry, his close scientific research, his literary labors, including many elaborate addresses, historical and biographical sketches, documents and reports on Educational and other important public subjects, all of which are valuable and deserve preservation. I commend this useful task to his accomplished and worthy son, LeRoy Stafford Boyd, of Washington City, who is in possession of abundant materials which relate to the history of his father, and has already shown himself to be well fitted to present that history in acceptable and durable form.

Born in 1834, at Wytheville, in the heart of the Virginia mountains, D. F. Boyd grew to manhood among brilliant companions and strong southern associations. His boyhood chum was Jeb Stuart, who afterwards became the most famous Confederate cavalry commander, of whom Colonel Boyd wrote a most graphic, sympathetic and delightful biography.

Graduating in 1856 with the degree of M. A. at the University of Virginia, young Boyd taught school for a year at his home town. In 1857, desiring to pursue the profession of civil engineering, he went to Marshall, Texas, for the purpose of procuring employment on the Pacific Railroad, which was then under construction.

But fate had other things in store for him. Meeting at Shreveport Judge W. B. Egan, a fellow Virginian, who had come to Louisiana with his distinguished father, Dr. Bartholomew Egan, and his equally distinguished brother, Doctor J. C. Egan, Boyd was induced to re-enter the profession of teaching, and accepted the principalship of the Homer High School, in Claiborne Parish. He subsequently became principal of a school at Rocky Mount, in Bossier Parish, where he was teaching in the summer of 1859, when he was elected Professor of Ancient Languages in the State Seminary of Learning at Alexandria, established by Act 317 of 1855, and organized by Act 228 of 1858, of the Statutes of Louisiana.

Boyd accepted his new position and went to work to equip the institution for successful operation. The school opened January the second, 1860, and in the first report, issued in July of that year, Boyd is put down as "Professor of Ancient Languages and English Literature." Evidently they had doubled his duties, but he never objected to a thing like that. The school had ample funds and a hundred fine cadets; but it was only a magnificent experiment. Its first Superintendent was William Tecumseh Sherman, a scholarly graduate of West Point, with more than fifteen years' experience in the Regular Army, highly accomplished and widely acquainted with the world and the affairs of men. Yet, from the very first, this able officer seemed to rely on Boyd and look to him to do all the hard work of the institution. This is shown by the Sherman-

Boyd letters, edited by LeRoy Stafford Boyd, and published in the Sunday Times-Democrat, of New Orleans, in the spring and summer of 1903. It was Boyd who superintended the laying off of the Seminary grounds. It was Boyd who directed the carpenters in their extensions and repairs. It was Boyd who made out a list of furniture for the class rooms and a list of books for the library. Sherman had discovered Boyd and his wonderful genius for work. Perhaps it would be better to say they had discovered each other. So when the hot season of 1860 had arrived and the first session of the Seminary had been successfully closed, and the manly cadets had gone to their happy homes, and the gallant superintendent and professors felt constrained to seek relief and recreation in cooler climes, Boyd volunteered to remain at the Seminary in charge of all the work of preparing for the coming session. That was just like Boyd; he always put himself last. He always took the hardest job and slept on the hardest bed.

On the 5th of August, 1860, Colonel Sherman, on the eve of departing for the North, wrote to Professor Boyd, appointing him acting superintendent of the Seminary until Sherman should return. Thus, this veteran officer entrusted all his powers and responsibilities to this young teacher of twenty-six, implying a confidence and esteem and trust as beautiful as they were remarkable.

The first Report of the Seminary, which was prepared by General Sherman, called attention to the fact that the School was established and supported by funds derived from lands granted by the General Government. This is true of the University as it exists to-day; it derives all its endowment and its valuable location, said to be worth half a million dollars, from the United States. In the shadow of such an Institution, it would be the grossest inconsistency for any one to oppose Federal aid to public education.

Let me dwell for a few moments on the picture of this young Virginian, out there in the quiet pine woods, working through the long hot days of August and September, keeping his lonely vigil, planning for the building of a great institution of learning for the whole Southwest. The spirit of the lofty pines breathed into his soul and the dream of his life began. Then and there he was annointed and consecrated for his life-work. Like Pygmalion, he fell in love with the beauty of his own grand thoughts, and, henceforth, there will be for him but one cause, one ambition, and one hope. Henceforth, the history of the Seminary will be his history. Its struggles and sufferings and defeats will be his struggles and sufferings and defeats. He will never falter, he will never give up, and, after a while, its glory, thank God, shall be his glory, though he be dead and gone.

But before he is ready to take up his great battle for the University, there is another act in his life's drama, another step in his development and preparation which I must not omit. When the Seminary unfurled its prosperous sails and was just starting on its beneficent voyage, the demon of war shook his dusky pinions over the land and all the business of civil life ceased. On the 14th of May, 1861, Boyd resigned and repaired with a number of cadets to Camp Moore, where he enlisted as a private in Company B of the Ninth La. Regiment. The members of this Regiment were exceedingly afraid they would not get to the front before the war was over. And so, bethinking themselves that Dick Taylor was a brother-in-law of President Davis and might secure the privilege of taking the regiment to Virginia in time to take part in the closing fight, they elected Taylor their Colonel. Sure enough he carried them at once to Richmond and completely satisfied their desire for fighting early and late, and plenty of it.

Boyd was appointed regimental commissary with the rank of Captain, and when Dick Taylor was made Brigadier General, he made Boyd his brigade commissary with the rank of Major. Boyd discharged the arduous duties of his position and also took part in the fighting all through Jackson's world-renowned Valley Campaign, until at Chancellorsville he saw the fall of that great mystic soldier whom he used to call Parson Stonewall. After that, Dick Taylor was assigned to the Trans-Mississippi Department and appointed Boyd on his staff as Chief of Engineers. Here he continued to serve on Red River until he was captured by Jay Hawkers who carried him to Natchez and sold him to the Federals for one hundred dollars. The Jay Hawkers treated him very roughly and almost took his life on several occasions, and in crossing Black River they upset the flat, apparently, for the purpose of drowning him. Being very active and a good swimmer, Boyd soon got on top of the upset flat and with his own hands saved two of his captors from drowning. He used to tell us that he enjoyed pulling the long whiskered sinners out of the water. He was a man who did not know how to harbor malice, resentment or revenge. At Natchez, Boyd was carried before General W. T. Sherman, and the two friends met for the first time after they separated at Alexandria. "Gentlemen," said Sherman, addressing those around him, "This is Professor D. F. Boyd. He calls himself a Major, but he is mistaken. He is Professor Boyd still." The upshot of the interview was that Sherman took Boyd to New Orleans where he was exchanged for three Federal officers who had been captured at Mansfield. Boyd got back to the Confederate Army with thirteen thousand dollars in his boot leg that he had on him at the time of his capture.

Dick Taylor having been assigned to a command east of the Mississippi River, Boyd actively served on the staff of General Brent for the rest of the war. He was a gallant soldier, true to the South, and his military experience strengthened the fibres of his character. He mingled intimately with the great soldiers of the Confederacy; he slept on the same blanket with Major Bob Wheat the night before he was killed, and saw that peerless soldier of fortune buried where he fell. He was the daily companion of General Dick Taylor, and often rode and talked with General Stuart. He knew and loved all the Virginia Generals, especially bluff old Jubal Early, whose thin high voice he was fond of imitating in telling us of a battle where every soldier on the Southern side was badly needed at the front. As Early rode forward he met an eloquent chaplain, moving rapidly in the opposite direction. "Where in the hell are you going?" "To the rear," said the breathless parson. "Yes," screamed General Early, "You are always talking about the joys of Heaven, and now you have a chance to get there pretty —— quick, you are running to the rear! Away with such religion!"

But of all the great Southern soldiers, the one that impressed and inspired and influenced Boyd the most was Robert E. Lee, the great central sun that rose above the horizon of the South, to shine forever more. He saw his fame grow and spread until it was co-terminous with the limits of the world, at once the greatest and the best of men, the mightiest soldier and the purest patriot combined. And when the war was over and Appomattox had become a part of history, he saw the noblest Virginian of them all lay aside the habiliments of power without a murmur or a sigh, and enter upon the duty of teaching the young men of the South. The peerless "Sword of Robert E. Lee" was changed into the teacher's wand, and up there in the Blue Ridge Mountains another transfiguration took place, a transfiguration of supreme devotion, while the angel of the South laid her hands upon his head and proclaimed, "This is my beloved son in whom I am well pleased."

And now the fullness of time had come for Colonel Boyd to take up the great burden and work of his life. He came out of the war with his love for the South stronger than ever and his convictions clearer than ever that the South's chief need was universal education. Before the War, public education was not popular in the South. Her school systems were imperfect and inefficient, and she learned, too late, in the red glare of battle, that this was a sad mistake. If there had been more public schools in the South, there would have been more skilled laborers. And if there had been more skilled laborers, there would have been more manufactures and better munitions of war. Colonel Boyd knew that the only hope for the South's future, the only salvation for her society and her commerce, the only remedy for all the evils and misfortunes that four years of unparallelled warfare brought upon her, was to be found in the liberal education of her young men. His heart burned within him to relieve the distress and gloom that covered the entire South. His zeal and love grew more fervent and made a finer tone, a higher octave in the music of his life.

When Boyd resigned his Professorship in 1861, the Board of Supervisors in their report of October 26th, 1861, referred to "David F. Boyd, Professor of Ancient Languages, whose unceasing and self-denying discharge of the most minute duties of his department had often attracted the notice and elicited the commendation of the Supervisors." Some of the Supervisors who had adopted this fine tribute were still on the board when the war ended, and, at their instance, Governor J. Madison Wells, in July, 1865, appointed Colonel D. F. Boyd Superintendent of the State Seminary of Learning and Military Academy. The buildings near Alexandria were being used by the Federals as an Army Hospital, but before the end of July, Boyd called on General Canby for possession. Somehow or other he got possession, and with amazing energy he restored and repaired the dilapidated institution so that he was ready to open school on the second of October, 1865. It took money to do this, and Boyd prevailed upon Governor Wells to borrow Twenty Thousand Dollars to run the school until the Legislature could meet. By Act 63, approved March 15th, 1866, the Legislature appropriated $25,800 to pay the interest on the Seminary Fund for the years 1863, 1864 and 1865, and provided that the $20,000 borrowed by the Governor should be paid out of this appropriation. This act also appropriated $5000 for library and philosophical apparatus, $5000 for repairs, and $15,600 for the maintenance and tuition of fifty-two beneficiary cadets. Colonel Boyd was the author of this act of the Legislature, and of every other statute referring to the State Seminary or State University, including the act which consolidated the State University with the Agricultural and Mechanical College in 1877.

Every meeting of the Legislature was a crisis for the school, and Boyd was the man who met every crisis and saved the school. In those days society in the South was in a state of upheaval. The embers of sectional hostility were still burning, and bloody riots were the order of the day. Yet, through it all, Boyd kept to the herculean task assumed by him, to build up a high institution of learning at the public expense. He placed in the Act of 1866 a clause requiring beneficiary cadets to teach two years after their graduation.

And thus he began to provide teachers of the highest grade for the schools of Louisiana. By Act 131, approved March 28th, 1867, he increased the beneficiary cadets from fifty-two to ninety-eight, with an appropriation of $400 a year for the maintenance and tuition of each cadet. In 1867 the Federal General ordered him to suspend military exercises in the Seminary. He applied to the Secretary of War and had the order revoked.

He had trouble enough in 1866 and 1867, but in 1868 a still darker struggle confronted him. A new Constitution had been established in Louisiana, under which more than two-thirds of the Legislators were negroes, and Article 135 of the Constitution provided that no separate schools should be created for the races. This was the most malicious clause in that Constitution, and it meant the complete ostracism of the Southern whites from the public schools of Louisiana. The problem that confronted Colonel Boyd was to preserve his school for the use and benefit of the young white men of the State, and yet to obtain support from Legislatures controlled by Carpetbaggers and negroes. To accomplish this delicate, and yet tremendous task, he found that he had to take a part in organizing the public school system of Louisiana. In this enterprise he had a staunch and unfaltering friend in Governor Henry Clay Warmoth, and he often declared, orally and in writing, that the Seminary would have perished had it not been for the friendship of Governor Warmoth, during each year of whose administration, from 1868 to 1872, the support of the institution was unfailing, generous and ample.

He had other friends in and outside of the Legislature, but his chief co-worker was Dr. J. C. Egan, who represented in that Legislature the 20th Senatorial District, composed of the Parishes of Bienville, Claiborne and Bossier. His distinguished and scholarly father, Doctor

Bartholomew Egan, the intimate friend of Jefferson, Madison and Monroe, and of other foremost men in American history, had, immediately after the close of the war, sacrificed the repose of his declining years to take an active part on the Board of Supervisors at Alexandria. It was Doctor Bartholomew Egan and General G. Mason Graham, another eminent and patriotic son of Virginia, who loved the Seminary as a child of his old age, and Judge W. A. Seay, scholar, jurist and statesman, and W. C. Black of New Orleans, who caused Governor Wells to appoint Boyd Superintendent in 1865. Doctor J. C. Egan was already bound to the Seminary by the strongest ties. He had been all through the war with Boyd. He was surgeon of the 9th Regiment in Virginia and Surgeon-General in Louisiana on Dick Taylor's staff when Boyd was Chief of Engineers. He and Boyd were kindred spirits, and when they met in the Louisiana Legislature, Boyd as Educator and Egan as Senator, a pair of noble brothers, they worked together for the holy cause of Southern education. Doctor Egan is one of the few surviving Senators of that turbulent period, and I have his personal assurance that to Colonel D. F. Boyd, more than to any other Southern man, was due the credit of organizing a public school system, in the Southern States, which gave separate schools and equal educational opportunities to the two races. I had the good fortune to obtain from Doctor Egan a written statement of Colonel Boyd's services in behalf of education during the period of Reconstruction. I shall publish this statement as a part of this address, for I regard it as the truest and best eulogy that could be paid Colonel Boyd. I know that every Alumnus will join me in thanking Doctor Egan and wishing that he may long be spared to this commonwealth, not only to mitigate the ills of humanity, by the employment of his great skill and knowledge, but to afford us a guide and bright example in the domain of pure patriotism, public virtue and stainless honor.

Boyd was the chief factor in avoiding the terrible alternative between mixed schools and no schools at all. Like all true people of the South, he believed that, as the slaves had been emancipated, they should be educated to better fit them for the duties of citizenship. He believed that ignorance among the blacks, as well as ignorance among the whites, is a menace to free government, and he promised the negroes in the Legislature that he would help them if they would help him. To avoid the pernicious provisions of the Constitution of 1868, he had inserted in Section 23 of Act 131 of 1869, and Section 25 of Act 6 of the Extra Session of 1870, the provision that "one or more public schools" should be taught in every school district, with the distinct understanding that one of those schools should be for white pupils and the other for colored pupils. By this simple device difficulties that seemed insurmountable were bridged over. A public school system for all classes was established, and the cause of education and civilization was preserved in the South. Let no one speak of the "starless night of reconstruction," for in that night of gloom the fairest star arose which ever shone above the horizon of Louisiana. It was the star of public education. The world long ago learned that it is unsafe to predict that nothing good can come out of Nazareth.

By Act 81 of the regular session of 1870, $35,000 was appropriated to Straight University, which was exclusively for the negro students, and provision was made for the education of one indigent pupil from each Parish. By such means, Egan and Boyd obtained munificent appropriations for the White Seminary at Baton Rouge. In 1869, in addition to the interest on the Seminary Fund, Boyd obtained $39,200 for the maintenance and tuition of ninety-eight beneficiary cadets. By Act 47, approved March 16th, 1870, written by Boyd, he secured an increase of the beneficiary cadets to one hundred and thirty-two, and an appropriation of $350 a year for the maintenance and tuition of each one of them. By this same Act, Colonel Boyd changed the name of the institution from the Louisiana State Seminary of Learning and Military Academy to the Louisiana State University. In 1872, by Act 22, the Louisiana State University received an appropriation of $46,200 for the support of the beneficiaries, and other appropriations, aggregating over $70,000 for that one year.

This was the last appropriation ever made by the State for the support of beneficiary cadets. Colonel Boyd always referred to the beneficiary system as "The handsomest feature of the institution." This system was begun by Act 317 of 1855, which established the Seminary of Learning at Alexandria, and provided for the maintenance and tuition of sixteen indigent young men. Act 228 of 1858 organized the school, changed its name to State Seminary of Learning, and provided for the same number of beneficiary cadets. But in March, 1860, when Sherman and Boyd had taken charge of the School, they jointly prepared Act 98 of that year, which incorporated the military features of West Point, changed the name to the Louisiana State Seminary of Learning and Military Academy, and increased the number of beneficiary cadets to fifty-two. Under Boyd's inspiration, the word "Indigent" disappeared from the Statute and it was enacted that the State Cadets should be put "On a footing of perfect equality with pay cadets." So you see that the beneficiary system originated before the war when the State of Louisiana was the richest commonwealth in the world, having an assessment of $1600 per caput of her population. At the close of the war, when Louisiana had become the poorest community on earth, Boyd kept up the beneficiary system, the only change in the Act of 1866 being the provision that these cadets should teach two years in the State Schools. In 1867, their number was increased to ninety-eight, and in 1870 to one hundred and thirty-two. This was Boyd's doing. Amid the wreck and ruin, the turbulence and confusion, the extravagance and peculation around him, his supreme effort was to save something for the State. From the very jaws of hell, he snatched a subsidy to educate hundreds of young men and thus became more than their intellectual father, for he was the creator of their minds.

It is not necessary to detail here the benefits and results of this beneficiary system. But if it were proper on this occasion to refer to personal experiences, I could tell the story of one State cadet, who came out from a little farm in the hills of Claiborne Parish down to Alexandria, almost dazzled by the opportunity to get an education, where he was made welcome by the kindly Superintendent with generous, glowing face, good grey eyes, commanding brow, serenely high, and firm and gentle hand that led him through the fields of science, and on up the heights of knowledge where shone the light that never failed on land or sea. And this is the story of all the beneficiary cadets. They realized then, as they know now, that one man alone stood between their school and destruction. They knew this after each meeting of the Legislature, and when the buildings at Alexandria were burned to the ground on the 15th of October, 1869, and the Cadets were drawn up in line before the smoking ruins, and heard the general order read to go home and hold themselves in readiness to return, the Cadets knew that Boyd would save the University. With the lightning speed of genius, he solved the problem, obtained the right to use part of the Deaf and Dumb Asylum at Baton Rouge, and by the first of November we received notice to come back to our studies.

But the Asylum could not be the permanent home of the University. A long and bitter struggle was made to prevent its continued use. Boyd had to make a fight in every Legislature to retain possession of the Asylum, but he knew that it was not the proper abiding place of the school. A determined effort was made to carry the University back to Alexandria, but Boyd was looking elsewhere. As early as March, 1870, he induced the Legislature to petition the Secretary of War to grant the temporary use of the Arsenal at Baton Rouge to the University. From that time forward he expended vast energy in the effort to secure the Federal Barracks and grounds. At last, in 1886, without the permission of the Government, and without authority from the Board of Supervisors, Boyd moved in and took possession of the Barracks and two hundred acres of land and turned it over to the University for a permanent home. Like Jefferson's Louisiana Purchase, this was a magnificent breach of the law, but it settled the question of a permanent seat for the University. In 1887 the Government granted the temporary use of the Barracks, and in 1892 Congress made the title full and final. These were the results of Boyd's initiative, and Louisiana owes as much to him as if he had made this splendid donation from his private pocket. The Board of Supervisors censured him for acting without their authority, and he resigned the office of President in the fall of 1886. But he knew that his work was well done.

In dealing with the United States authorities Colonel Boyd was aided in a large measure by the warm friendship of General Sherman, and right here let me make record of the beautiful friendship that existed between these two men, as deep and trusting as the friendship of Jonathan and David. I am not the eulogist of Sherman; for I was born in Georgia where he illustrated all too well his blunt and brutal maxim, that "war is hell." But his friendship for Boyd reflects redeeming traits in his character. Like many notable friends in history, they were very different in many things.

With Sherman success was the test of merit; with Boyd, right was the only guide of action. Sherman fought to win, Boyd to do his duty. Sherman consulted self interest, Boyd was prompted by sentiment. Sherman loved the Union because it was great and powerful; Boyd loved the South because she was beautiful and true and noble. Sherman was a liberalized Puritan; Boyd was a broad Cavalier. But both of them were patriots : both were spotless in their integrity, both believed in a precise and faithful discharge of public and private obligations, both had the spirit of good fellowship in them and felt the glow of friendship's kindly flame. They loved each other before the war and during the war, and after the war, and showed how unnecessary a thing the Civil War was, and how worse than useless was the long sectional bitterness that followed it. Boyd was not the protegé of Sherman, as some have said; they were friends, two great, earnest, tolerant men, who clasped hands after the war and worked together to uplift the desolated South. No grander picture than that can be found in the annals of history on this planet. Perhaps, it would not be too much to say that Sherman's favor to the Louisiana State Seminary benefited the cause of education in the whole South; for Sherman's influence was powerful, if not paramount, with national and state governments, in those days.

Boyd did not work only to secure a home for the University. From the very first he had his eye on the appropriation made by Congress in 1862 of a large quantity of land, to establish an agricultural and mechanical college in every State in the Union. As early as 1867 Boyd urged upon the Legislature the importance of obtaining these lands, and through his influence a special agent was finally sent to Washington, who procured land scrip, which was sold and the proceeds invested in $335,000.00 of State bonds. In his report for 1874, Colonel Boyd made an unanswerable argument in favor of combining the two funds which had been given by the general government to the State, in the support of one broad literary and industrial institution, on the ground that the education of the mind and the hand and the heart succeeds best in one combined institution. The Kellogg government turned a deaf ear to his pleadings and established the Agricultural and Mechanical College at Chalmette, in St. Bernard Parish. This did not discourage Boyd. He marshalled all the powers of inexorable logic, he called to his aid all the leading educators of the country, he employed all the resources of importunate zeal, until his very heart beats wore away all opposition, and in 1876 he secured, from a hostile Legislature, the passage of Act 145, written by himself, uniting the two institutions and giving birth to the Louisiana State University and Agricultural and Mechanical College, realizing his dream of a great central institution, with co-ordinated departments, embracing all branches of learning and all forms of art and industry, the keystone of the educational arch in the State.

But Kellogg would not sign this act. His Secretary of State would not promulgate it, and it would have slept the sleep of death had not its author kept guard over it, until, under a new administration, he secured its promulgation and publication. In 1877, the Board of Supervisors, presided over by Governor Nicholls, elected Colonel Boyd President of the consolidated institution, and he assumed the arduous task of putting it into working shape. Surely now, under a new and better regime, he might expect some little respite from his toils. But this was not to be. The fight against the University was renewed in the Constitutional Convention of 1879, and Colonel Boyd had to confront a hostile Committee on Education, whose chairman was filled with the idea that the State University at Baton Rouge would destroy the University at New Orleans. In this Convention, Boyd again saved the University. They cut down the principal and interest of both funds that had been granted by the Federal Government, but they recognized the perpetuity of the University and recommended it to the generosity of the Legislature. Here was another "victory of endurance born."

Boyd could not make all these fights without making many enemies. Soon after the adoption of the Constitution of 1879, some of these enemies found lodgment in the University and the Board of Supervisors removed Colonel Boyd from the Presidency, pretending to base their action on his financial management. His Report for 1875 accounted for every dollar of all the appropriations made to the University, and showed that the deficit was due to the depreciation of State warrants, which amounted, in six years, to $132,000.00. In 1882, both Houses of the Louisiana Legislature appointed a joint committee to investigate Colonel Boyd's accounts. Doctor R. L. Luckett of Rapides was Chairman of the Senate Committee; the House Committee Chairman was Judge W. A. Seay of Shreveport. After a thorough investigation, these committees unanimously reported that Boyd's accounts were scrupulously correct, and that his financial administration had been able and faithful. They further reported that the removal of Colonel Boyd from the Presidency was without cause, and had been brought about by a combination of parties, some on the inside and some on the outside of the institution, for the purpose of getting control of the University, or destroying it altogether. This emphatic and conclusive vindication of Colonel Boyd was followed in 1884 by his unanimous re-election as President. But even this did not silence the enemies he had made. I will not lend significance to those enemies by giving their names or motives. Let them sleep in the obscurity to which indulgent fate has consigned them. Their attacks, for the most part covert, were compounded of one part prejudice and two parts ignorance, one of them being that his religious ideas were too broad. He made no more claim to superior piety than did Abou Ben Adheim; he was simply "one who loved his fellowmen." What if he stood without the Temple, afar off, and prayed, with bowed head and scarcely audible voice, "God be merciful to me, a sinner." That is the only kind of holiness justified by the divine Nazarene. Colonel Boyd could not be a sectarian, nor could he help it if University Education has a fatal tendency to destroy inherited ideas and habits of religion.

But, as far as lay in his power, from first to last, he filled the minds of his pupils with ideals of reverence, morality, honor and manhood. These ideals permeated his conception of true and virtuous education so that he put them in all his Reports and embodied them in Section 3 of Act 145 of 1876, defining the scope of this institution, which, he provided, "Shall have for its object to become an institution of learning, in the broadest and highest sense, where literature, science, and all the arts may be taught; where the principles of truth and honor may be established, and a noble sense of personal and patriotic and religious duty inculcated; in fine, to fit the citizen to perform justly, skillfully, and magnanimously all the offices, both private and public, of peace and war." Was there ever a nobler outline of the scope and purposes of a perfect education?

Some educators, like Horace Mann, have advocated State education as a good investment, because it pays in dollars and cents, in the increased skill and earning capacity which it gives to the citizen. There are other educational philosophers, like Herbert Spencer, who hold that the true object of education is to elevate the individual, developing all the faculties and evolving the strongest and best specimens of mankind. Colonel Boyd combined both these theories in his conception of public education. He wanted to train his pupils to become useful citizens of the South, to utilize her boundless material resources and make her the richest, as she is the most beautiful land on earth. To this end, he taught that labor with the hand is as honorable as labor with the brain. He taught that practical common sense is the best capital in any vocation, and he warned us that the prodigy of the school often becomes a pigmy in the world.

As an offset to Millet's gloomy picture of "The man with the hoe," he pointed us to "The man with the engine;" with erect form and intellectual brow, with hope and courage and triumph written in every lineament of his beaming face. That was the sort of man, with trained eye and hand and muscle, in whose keeping Boyd wished to place the destiny of the South. His ideas of industrial reform were broad, concrete and intensely practical, and made each industrial pupil an apprentice in the State's workshop.

But Colonel Boyd also looked upon education from a more than utilitarian point of view. He wanted to make skilled workmen and good citizens. But above everything, he wanted to make gentlemen out of his pupils; and to him the term "gentleman" meant the highest type of man, a man who loved his country and mankind, but loved truth and justice and duty most of all. He drilled into the mind of every boy Shakespeare's superb maxim :

"To thine own self be true,
And it must follow as the night the day
Thou can'st not then be false to any man."

He gave an ethical turn to every branch of learning, and found in education the essence of all moral and social advancement.

No account of Colonel Boyd's qualities as a teacher would be complete without mention of the enthusiasm which he carried into every class-room and imparted to every student. He became one of the Cadets without losing his dignity. He was the most approachable and the most optimistic of men. He taught that life is worth living and happiness is the inalienable right, as it is the universal desire of every living thing. From the lowest to the highest ranges of creation, everything is yearning and struggling and reaching out for life. Every grace of form and motion, every tint of beauty, every touch of loveliness, is a chord in the mighty joy of existence and the throbbing aspiration of organic and inorganic nature to ascend in the scale of being. The love of life is the most powerful passion of humanity. Every sigh of love, every emotion of tenderness, every tear of pity dropped into the untimely grave, and all the myriad devices to prolong existence, sanitation, surgery, and "the divine art of healing," are testimonies all to the insatiable longing for life. Life is the supreme condition, the indispensable element, the priceless boon, and it is the momentous mission of the educator to prepare men to extract the purest and highest and fullest happiness from this boon of life. That is the meaning of all the temples of learning and all the hosts of education. The tree of life grows hard-by the tree of knowledge, and happiness is the taste of their blended fruit.

Knowledge is power. Knowledge is wealth. Knowledge is beauty. Knowledge is happiness. Knowledge is the wing whereby we fly to heaven. It solves every problem. It unravels every mystery. It unfolds the secrets of old earth like the pages of a book and gives its proper number to every chapter, section and paragraph. It is the lever that moves a million worlds, and sets them spinning, like tops, in the orbits of space. The gods have already said that knowledge makes man "like one of us," and some day knowledge will scale the garden walls of Eden and push aside the flaming sword and the Cherubim that keep the way to the tree of life.

Therefore, the diffusion of knowledge, the teacher's true vocation, becomes the mightiest business of this life and the immeasurable source of happiness for mankind.

Happiness may be found in the haven of peace, or on the rocking billows of the storm. It may be found on the misty mountain top, or in the lowest vale of life, in success or in defeat, in fame or in obscurity, in the garb of grandeur or in the sanbenito of the victim at the stake. But while Boyd taught us that happiness can be found in every walk and stage of life, he taught it must always be found in the service of others and the path of duty. He was filled with an indomitable alacrity to serve others, and his whole being was attuned to the sublime optimism of the Sermon on the Mount, which bestows all the beatitudes on the poor and the lowly, the proscribed and the persecuted. But duty was his highest watchword, duty the key to right living and to right teaching, duty the surest guide and sweetest reward; stern, yet beautiful; firm, yet gentle; not only "the sublimest word in the English language," but also the passport to supremest happiness, in all the worlds and in all the cycles of time.

> "Stern law-giver! Yet thou dost wear
> The Godhead's most benignant grace;
> Nor know we anything so fair
> As is the smile upon thy face;
> Flowers laugh before thee on their beds
> And fragrance in thy footsteps treads;
> Thou dost preserve the stars from wrong;
> And the most ancient heavens, through thee,
> are fresh and strong."

If ever a man lived who was hypnotized by his faith in the ultimate triumph of the right, it was D. F. Boyd. It was this faith that made him undergo incredible toils and privations. Let no one imagine that he clung to his position at the head of the University from necessity or vanity. In 1873, when all Legislative support had been withdrawn from the University and the State Cadets had been disbanded, he was offered honorable and lucrative positions in other States, which he declined. For four years he was deprived of all revenue, and it seemed inevitable that the institution must go down. In 1875 he was offered by the Khedive of Egypt the Superintendency of the Egyptian Military College, with the rank and pay of Brigadier General, and he was urged by family and friends to accept, but he did not waver. He wrote to Governor Kellogg in July, 1875, that he would go to Egypt only on one condition, which was that he could be assured, before leaving, of the continued existence and safety of the University. To save the University, that was his life-work, and no day was too dark and no task was too hard for him to carry out that work. Perhaps the climax of his sufferings and sacrifices was reached in 1874. I wish that I had time to give some extracts from the diary which Colonel Boyd kept during the summer of that year. Deserted by friends, hounded by acrimonious lawsuits, without professors, without the means to pay for the necessaries of life, almost starving, with threadbare garments, he did not forget that he was upholding the banner of Southern education in the darkest hour that ever threatened her civilization. He tells the story of this terrible ordeal in his private diary, and every page of it burns with the fire of self-devotion. It is a story of struggle and suffering, of poverty and sorrow, of privation and pain, of foiled efforts and hopes deferred, but it is, also, a story of undying faith and trust and confidence in the right. If there was a man in the Nineteenth Century entitled to enter the "noble army of martyrs," it was David French Boyd. He trod the wine press alone; he sounded all the depths and shoals of sorrow; he tasted of the bitter cup of defeat, and like the noble stag that is pulled down in the race, he heard the sleuth-hounds bay their fiercest notes of triumph around his fallen form. He was not the only one in history who could save others, but could not help himself.

But let us lose no pity on the man who suffers for a good cause. He has sources of delight that the world knows not of. Take not one single thorn out of the Martyr's Crown, for every bleeding wound will turn into a fountain of eternal bliss. Take not the bitter cup away from the lips of heroic love, for every drop shall turn into the nectar of Olympic joy!

But it has all come out right, and to-day he triumphs above all other Louisianans; above Senators, Generals, Governors and Presidents, we place this monument to-day.

Honors are sometimes paid to living men by those who expect help from them—"mouth honor, breath, which the poor heart would fain refuse by dare not." But when a man is dead and shut up in the tomb, when he lies out yonder in the hushed stillness of Magnolia Cemetery, with no power to reward or respond, O then it is that honor counts! Then it is that the homage of the heart is pure and undefiled and words of praise fall like the gentle rain from Heaven, helping him who gives and him who receives.

As you go up from Boston Commons, in front of the State House, you behold two statues, one of Daniel Webster, the other of Horace Mann. Massachusetts does well to place her greatest educator side by side with her greatest statesman, and we of Louisiana do better, at this time, to assign our greatest educator to the highest niche in our Hall of Fame. No one can stand in the Vatican and gaze upon the immortal struggle of the Laoccoon, see the calm dignity with which the father "consents to death yet conquers agony," and behold him strain every muscle to succor the young even in the moment of dissolution, no one can look upon that heroic spectacle without feeling the heart leap up and resolving to think more exalted thoughts and do more exalted deeds. Before such a scene, everything seems possible to us, and we know that we are immortal because of the thrilling emotions which we feel in the presence of a noble deed.

And so we raise this Memorial Hall in order that the contemplation of tireless labors, splendid public virtue and colossal courage may uplift and guide the youths of this and coming generations. His memory will inspire higher standards of public and private life. His example will have power to redeem human nature from littleness and sordidness. We commemorate Colonel D. F. Boyd because he was the benefactor of this State and of the entire South. We commemorate him because he fulfilled the Miltonic definition of conspicuous greatness:

"When great things of small
Useful of hurtful, prosperous of adverse,
We can create, and in what place soe'er,
Thrive under evil and work ease out of pain
Through labor and endurance."

We commemorate him because he was greater than Carnegie, greater than Vanderbilt, greater than Rockefeller, for he founded a great University without money, and endowed it with his radiant soul!

Oh, if his spirit could speak to us to-day, he would tell us that the only monument he ever desired was to be loved and cherished in the hearts of his old Cadets.

He would say to us: "Be worthy sons of the South and build up her waste places. Fling away ambition! Fling away all self-seeking! Dare to be faithful, dare to be true; dare to be just to all men and that will be a dearer monument to me than lasting brass or the regal seat of the Pyramids." May I not reply to him?—in the name of the Alumni, I will reply to him: Friend and teacher! philanthropist and philospher! soldier and statesman, true hearted gentleman! To-day we acknowledge our indebtedness to thee! Thou didst widen the bounds of life for us. Thou didst teach us that life is sweet and death itself is sweet when we die at the post of duty. Thou wast the foremost apostle of Southern education and didst give thy life to bring the University within the reach of poor Southern boys. And to-day we congratulate thy enfranchised spirit that thy life-work is marching on. The mountain ranges of difficulty that thou didst climb have fallen away. The path that thou didst mark with bruised feet has grown easy. A thousand eager champions now rush forward to seize the banner of Southern enlightenment. A thousand beacons of education throw their prophetic effulgence across the coming destiny of the South. And thanks to the campaign which thou didst inaugurate, O hero of a glorious cause, slowly but surely,

"Out of the shadows of night,
The South rolls into light,
It is day-break everywhere!"

APPENDIX.

STATEMENT OF DR. J. C. EGAN.

Hon. DAVID F. BOYD.

The subject of this notice graduated at the University of Virginia in 1856, and came South with the view of getting employment as Civil Engineer, on the then contemplated Southern Pacific Railroad, which had been chartered and was being constructed from Savannah, on parallel 32½, to the Pacific Coast, as we then thought below the snow shed. A portion of that line was being constructed from Monroe to the Mississippi River, and from Shreveport to the Texas Line, west, and Texas had been appealed to for grants for the construction in that great Territory. Everything, however, was in abeyance, and my brother, Judge W. B. Egan, meeting Boyd in Marshall, Texas, seeking employment, induced him to visit Homer, in Claiborne Parish, for the purpose of establishing a High School, which was conducted by him successfully for some time. He was then induced to take a school in the neighborhood of Rocky Mount, in Bossier Parish, among a wealthy community, where he also succeeded in building up a school of high grade.

Judge Egan being a member of the Board of Supervisors of the State Seminary and Military Academy, then located in the pine woods north of Alexandria, a few miles, which was then in charge of W. T. Sherman as Superintendent, with the concurrence of those who knew Boyd's value, had him appointed one of the Professors in that Institution, which he filled successfully until the breaking out of the war when Sherman went North, and Boyd, with a number of the young gentlemen of the Institution, came to Camp Moore, at Tangipahoa, in Washington Parish, and enlisted in the 9th Louisiana Regiment, which was organized with

Richard Taylor, as Colonel, E. G. Randolph, of Bossier Parish, as Lieutenant Colonel, and H. B. Walker, as Major. The regiment was immediately sent to Virginia, and when the Louisiana Brigade was organized, Boyd was made Brigade Commissary, in which capacity he served until General Taylor was made a Major General, and sent to the command of the District of West Louisiana, with his headquarters at Alexandria, when he applied to Boyd to take a position on his staff as Chief Engineer. Boyd took an active part in the building of the various forts along Red River, and was at one time captured by Jay-Hawkers and carried across the country to Natchez. An incident happened on that trip which I will mention to show the character of the man. They crossed Black River, near Trinity, on a raft which sunk, and one of the old gray headed Jay-Hawkers was about to sink when Boyd grabbed his gray locks and pulled him to shore. He reached Natchez, where, it is said, the Jay-Hawkers received one hundred dollars for his capture. His name was sent up to the commander, who happened to be W. T. Sherman, his old chief in the State Seminary and Military Academy, who immediately sent for him to be brought to his quarters. Boyd's relation of that interview was quite amusing. When he walked in, Commodore Porter was sitting in conversation with Sherman, who was leaning on the mantel and talking very earnestly, and when Boyd was ushered in, Sherman grabbed him by both hands and exclaimed, "How do you do, Prof. Boyd! I am very glad to see you, indeed, sir! Very glad, indeed, sir! Commodore Porter, this is Prof. Boyd, one of my assistants in the State Seminary and Military Academy of Louisiana. He is Prof. Boyd. He calls himself Major. He is no such thing. He is Prof. Boyd, sir." He then said, "Boyd, what in the Hell am I going to do with you? They tell me I have got to send them all up yonder to Fort Douglas." Boyd said, "Well, I reckon I will have to take my fate,

General, with the balance of those captured." Sherman said, "Sit down here and stay with me. I will guard you." Boyd remained with him, and Sherman said, "Look here, Boyd, I don't want to send you up yonder. Tell you what I'm going to do. I am going down to New Orleans,"—Butler was in New Orleans at the time—"and I will take you along with me down there and turn you over." "Just sit down and make yourself comfortable." Well, when Sherman went down and turned him over to Butler, he was put in one of those big compress prisons, and after the battle of Mansfied, Boyd was exchanged for 2 or 3 of the staff officers that had been captured there, and was sent up to Alexandria to receive those officers when they were being sent down by steamboat. I recall his providing a good dinner at our mess-hall. I went with him to receive them there and give them a good feed on their way. During all of this time of his capture and confinement in New Orleans, he had thirteen thousand dollars in his boot leg, that he had gotten to pay off the soldiers at Fort DeRusie, and brought it back all safe.

At the reorganization of the State Seminary and Military Academy, after the war, my father, Dr. Bartholomew Egan, was a member of the Board of Supervisors, and he, with the co-operation of General J. Mason Graham, Judge W. E. Seay, W. C. Black of New Orleans, and other Supervisors, induced the Military Governor, Mat. Wells, to have Boyd appointed as Superintendent of that Institution. He thus commenced his career as the head of, what was then, the State School, patterned after West Point.

Soon succeeding this period came the days of Reconstruction, when Warmoth was made Governor with the good old negro, Oscar J. Dunn, as Lieutenant Governor. It so happened that I was a member of the Reconstruction Senate of that period. All of the true people of Louisiana believed that as the slaves were emancipated, they should be educated, if they were to be fitted for free government at all, and of the measures that could be accomplished by a few true men of that legislative period, educational interest was one of the most prominent. There was no greater advocate or more effective and efficient co-operator in that movement than Col. David F. Boyd, and perhaps to him, more than any other Southern man, is due the credit of inaugurating the free school system, which allowed one or more schools in each District, which had in view the purpose of keeping the whites and blacks separate, and which eliminated from the control of the Superintendent of Public Education any control over the State Seminary and Military Academy which had been otherwise provided for by a Board of Supervisors. The first step necessary was to gain the influence and confidence of the Legislators, both white and black, by an earnest effort to advance the interest of the State along educational lines without bringing upon us the untoward consequences which would follow an attempt at mixed schools.

There happened to be placed on the Senate Committee on Education, as Chairman, a highly educated and accomplished Carpet Bagger (as we termed them in those years), the Hon. Hugh J. Campbell, who was familiar with the methods laid down by the Mass. Law on Public Education, of which the Hon. Horace Mann was the author, and which had been applied in some of those Western States from which he came. With his support, and by assisting the Colored People in all of their enterprises presented for our support, we finally secured their co-operation in voting on all measures for our own race without conflict or clash. The Reconstruction Superintendent of Public Education, the Hon. Mr. Conway, a Baptist Minister, who had been Chaplain of a Negro Regiment, had prepared a bill, unwieldy and impracticable, and upon consultation, we decided to get all of those interested in the subject of Education, white and black, including the President of "Straight University," and the colored teachers in the State who were accessible, in a conference with the joint committee of the Senate and House on Education, to consider and prepare a Free School System for the State of Louisiana. In that Assembly was read this omnibus bill of Conway's, which was repudiated by all parties present of both races. Then the bill prepared by Campbell, patterned by the Horace Mann bill, which provided for one or more schools in each District, and leaving the State Seminary and Military Academy entirely without any interference on the part of the Superintendent of Public Education or Public School Board, was finally adopted. This was accomplished by the co-operation of all classes for the cause of education, in which Col. Boyd took a more active part and was more influential than any other Southern man, and we were prepared for the events that follow.

The State Seminary Building, of which Col. Boyd was Superintendent, burned at a time when he had a large number of young gentlemen in his care. He came to New Orleans immediately, and got permission of the State Authorities to occupy the Institution at Baton Rouge, which was built for the blind and deaf and dumb of the State, which he got without any difficulty, and soon moved his State Seminary and Military Academy to that beautiful building which overlooks the Mississippi River, the few deaf and dumb and blind being provided with suitable quarters elsewhere.

Then came the conception by him, which was accepted by us all, of creating a State University, to include the State Seminary and Military feature and the Agricultural and Mechanical School, for which an appropriation had been authorized to each State by the National Congress, with the co-operation of the Educational Committee of the House and Senate, and especially the co-operation of the Hon. Hugh J. Campbell, L. A. Wilkes, of the Lower House, F. C. Zachary, and all of the true men of the Senate, which were very few in number, we were enabled to have prepared, first, a bill changing the name of the State Seminary and Military Academy to the State University, and incorporating with it the two above mentioned branches. Also providing for a topographical, geological and botanical survey of the State, by the authority and under the control of the State University, when so created. Also providing for the appointment of the Hon. Jno. Lynch, a Carpet Bagger from Ohio, who was a classmate of Cox, the then Secretary of the Interior, and make an appropriation of one thousand dollars for his expenses for the purpose of securing a grant for the Agricultural and Mechanical School. All of these measures being submitted to the Educational Committees, and meeting their approval, went before the Legislature for final adoption.

Now came the tug of war to find time to bring them before each branch of the Legislature for final passage. In the closing days of my history as a legislator, by agreement, that grand old character, Dr. Day, Senator from the Baton Rouge District, took his position by Oscar J. Dunn, the president of the Senate, and I went to the Lower House and occupied a position by the side of the Speaker, Mortimer Carr, who had all of the bills brought to his desk that I desired passed, and I had on the floor of the House, W. E. Dewes, who claimed to represent my Parish, Bienville, in front of the Speaker, who put all of the necessary motions for suspending the rules and passing from one reading to the other, and as it was passed, a special messenger was sent by the Speaker of the House, with that bill to Dr. Day, who had his emergency man in the Senate, and by agreement with the Hon. Oscar Dunn, President of Senate, had all those re-enacted by the Senate with the same unanimity.

Thus was accomplished Boyd's grand conception of a State School at the Capital, the grand results of which are obvious to all at this day, and which may be perpetuated for generations to come.

Then came the question of a domicile, and there Boyd showed his tact and grand magnetic power over those with whom he had been, in the course of his life, thrown in contact. Through Gen. Sherman's co-operation, it was he, almost unaided, who secured the present domicile of the University, which in former days was the United States Barracks.

Now came the trouble of building up the University under the adverse circumstances of Reconstruction time. All of the funds originally contributed by the National Government, for the sustenance of the State Seminary and Military Academy, and also, when obtained, for the Agricultural and Mechanical School, were invested in State securities which depreciated in value as time went on in the latter years of the administration of Warmoth and the period of Kellogg's rule as Governor, until the source of revenue had lessened to about one-third of their original value; yet, through it all, Boyd maintained the school and educated large numbers of youths of the State, many of whom are among the first and most prominent citizens of Louisiana. The Board of Supervisors of that day shared with him, as far as possible, the work of maintaining and developing the Institution. The means of public transportation were by steamboat or stage from the northern portion of Louisiana, and some of us would, at times, have to travel by way of Jackson, Miss., or Galveston, Tex., in order to attend a meeting of the Board of Supervisors. Under all difficulties, Boyd had the one unselfish idea of building the great State University, which we now see so happily resulting from those efforts. His removal of the Institution to its present domicile was even unauthorized by the then Board of Supervisors, although there were some men on the Board who sanctioned the step—Judge Sutherlin, Rev. Spearing, Judge Strickland and Sparks being among the number that I know.

It was my privilege to know, more intimately perhaps than any one else living at that period, Col. David F. Boyd, his aims and objects and his conception of his duty in this life to his fellow-man. His whole conception of life was that he had been placed here by his Creator to elevate and advance, as far as in his power lay, the human family, and bring them as near to the pattern given us in the character of our Savior, as possible. By his magnetic influence and kind, gentle and often affectionate manner, he seemed to have the power of drawing all with whom he came in contact to him, and intuitively discovering anything good and loyal in those whom he thus attached to him. In that way he was pre-eminently fitted for the training of the young. It was his constant and only aim to develop the best in every youth with whom he came in contact and to lead him to a true conception of his duties in life, thus making *a gentleman*, in the true sense of that word, of all of the youths under his care. Whilst the Military feature was continued in the Institution, it was not by strict Military rule that he governed, but by cultivating the self-respect of his students, thus leading them to be ashamed to do anything that a gentleman should not do.

J. C. EGAN, M. D.

SHREVEPORT, LA., Sept. 15, 1903.

Printed by Libri Plureos GmbH in Hamburg, Germany